A HEART FOR OBEDIENCE

A *Heart* FOR OBEDIENCE

JOY P. GAGE

VICTOR BOOKS ®
A DIVISION OF SCRIPTURE PRESS PUBLICATIONS INC.
USA CANADA ENGLAND

This study guide is based on the *Authorized (King James) Version*. Unless otherwise indicated, Scripture quotations are taken from this version.

Recommended Dewey Decimal Classification: 222.15
Suggested Subject Heading: BIBLE STUDY—DEUTERONOMY

Library of Congress Card Catalog Number: 87-062492
ISBN: 0-89693-421-7

VICTOR BOOKS
A division of SP Publications, Inc.
        Wheaton, Illinois 60187

CONTENTS

"Our speaker this evening has but thirty days to live . . ."

Imagine the audience response to such a statement. Imagine the curiosity aroused. What kind of speech can we anticipate from a man who knows he is in his last thirty days?

In a sense, Deuteronomy is such a speech. Moses was in the last month of his life when he delivered the message of this book to the Israelites. After having wandered for forty years because of their sin at Kadesh-barnea, the people were now about to occupy the land. The disobedient generation had died in the wilderness. Nothing remained to prevent the entry.

Joshua, as Moses' successor, would soon assume command, and Moses would climb to the top of Mount Pisgah and die without entering the Promised Land. Moses knew this. Joshua knew it. The people knew it.

The scene which unfolds in the opening passage of Deuteronomy may best be described as a pause for preparation. Standing between the past and the future the people pause, ready to go, waiting the final instructions. These instructions constitute the Book of Deuteronomy.

The first five verses of the book establish the location, the time frame, and the content of the message to be delivered. In his commentary on the Book of Deuteronomy (*The New International Commentary on the Old Testament*), P.C. Craigie comments on this crucial moment in which Moses rehearses past events to emphasize the importance of the present. "[Israel's] past history had been leading, within the plan and promise of God, to a future goal. But that future goal was contingent upon the obedience and commitment of the Israelites to their God."

Moses calls upon the record of the past and looks ahead to the future as he expounds the law. He has three recurring themes:

□ *In prosperity, remember God is the source of all blessings.*

□ *If you disobey God, remember He will discipline you.*

□ *In the tribulation which will surely follow disobedience, remember God will restore the repentant one who calls on Him.*

The word forgive does not appear in Deuteronomy, but God's forgiveness permeates the book. Moses cautioned Israel that they had not earned this land by their own greatness. God had given them this land because of His great love for them. And all He required was that they obey Him.

Moses repeatedly reminded the people that the future holds the potential for God's blessings or God's discipline. The choice is theirs. Obedience, a key word in the book, is a determining factor. Obedience was the key to entering the land. Obedience would be the key to remaining in the land.

To fully appreciate Deuteronomy it is necessary to visualize this pause for preparation not just from Israel's perspective, but also from Moses' perspective. Israel stood at a crucial juncture between the past and the future. But for Moses, time was running out. Ever since Meribah (Num. 20), Moses had known that he would die before the nation crossed over Jordan. At Meribah Moses had disobeyed God and as a consequence of that disobedience he was denied the privilege of leading the people into the land. Thus at the pause for preparation, we see Moses, a man whose days were numbered, earnestly seeking to prepare the people to enter a land to which he could not go.

What attitudes characterized Moses? Was he bitter? Did he rationalize his single act of disobedience against Israel's pattern of disobedience? Did he show anger toward them for what they had put him through?

In fact, Deuteronomy shows none of these attitudes. What we see is a man devoid of bitterness, a man who is preoccupied with the person of God. We see a man who continued to serve and to worship God until the day he died.

If you keep this perspective in mind, Deuteronomy will become more than a book of history, more than a sermon on the law. It will become a guide for today. It will show you the joy of obedience and the path for developing *a heart for obedience.*

Using This Study Guide
Deuteronomy is one of the Old Testament books of history. To study it properly you must read longer passages and pay close attention to historical details—what happened and who was involved. As you read, keep track of the actions that occur, and note particularly how the various characters responded to God's actions in their lives. By their examples, positive and negative, we gain principles for living today.

Familiarize yourself with the various sections of the chapters. Each study begins with Discovery Time, a personal study which develops observation, interpretation, and application skills.

Moments of Decision is a very personal application feature that is not meant to be shared in a group setting. This journaling exercise will give you the opportunity to "talk to the Lord" about what you have learned in the study and narrative sections. Some basic questions will be asked in this section, but these are just to get you started if you need help. Think of your journal as your private decision time.

The Digest section is provided as a commentary on the theme for the week. Read it after you have completed the personal study. If you are using this guide for group study, underline anything you do not understand and ask for clarification. Make a note of additional thoughts you may have which will add to the group discussion on this lesson.

Diversify is a resource section for all who wish to lead a group through these studies This section offers practical suggestions for enriching the group time. The guide provides specific instructions for each chapter of the study. Draw on these, but feel free to adapt, add, or change them according to the needs of your group.

CHAPTER ONE

Heart Patterns

🔊 DISCOVERY TIME 🔊

1. Read Deuteronomy 1:19-36, noting the facts of the incident. In Deuteronomy, Moses is looking back 40 years and recounting the incident at Kadesh-barnea. Numbers 13:26–14:11 records the incident as it happened. While many of the same details are included, Numbers gives some additional detail.

   Read Numbers 14:4-11, noting further facts of the incident. Close your eyes and think through what you have read, reconstructing the incident in your mind. Include as many details as you can remember.

   What negative actions do you find in the following verses?

   Deuteronomy 1:26

   Deuteronomy 1:27

   Numbers 14:10

2. In your own words, rephrase Deuteronomy 1:28, showing how the Israelites blamed someone else for their disobedience.

3. Moses reminds the Israelites of God's record of faithfulness which they discounted by disbelief (1:32). List the specific examples of God's faithfulness cited in these verses:

   Deuteronomy 1:30

   Deuteronomy 1:31

   Deuteronomy 1:33

4. Read the following verses and note in each the progression from attitude to action in Israel's disobedience.

   Numbers 14:1

   Numbers 14:2

Numbers 14:3

Numbers 14:4

Numbers 14:10 (see vv. 5-9)

5. What were the consequences of Israel's disobedience?

Deuteronomy 1:35

Numbers 14:22-23

Numbers 14:32-33

Numbers 14:36-37

6. Additional evidence of Israel's rebellious nature is seen in Numbers 14:40-44. After God made clear the consequences of disobedience, the Israelites further disobeyed by presumptuously proceeding to

the Promised Land when God had said stay in the wilderness. Because God was not with them, they were turned back by their enemies.

Disobedience always brings consequences; however, it is evident from Old Testament examples that there is a difference between disobeying and becoming characterized by disobedience. A person characterized by disobedience not only continually disobeys, he rationalizes action, discounts God's faithfulness, questions God's purpose, and stubbornly persists in having his own way.

Read the following verses and contrast Moses' act of disobedience with Israel's pattern of disobedience. Note *how* Moses disobeyed; the *consequences* of his disobedience; and his *response* to the consequences.

Numbers 20:7-11

Numbers 20:12

Deuteronomy 1:37

Deuteronomy 3:24-25

7. Deuteronomy 3:27–4:1 gives additional detail on Moses' response. In contrast to the Israelites who were characterized by disobedience, Moses did not rationalize his sin, question God's care for him, or forge presumptuously ahead when God said "No."

The phrases "so" (3:29) and "now therefore listen" (4:1) give us clues to Moses' attitude toward God's judgment of his sin. He accepted God's decision, proceeded to obey, and encouraged Israel to learn from his experience.

What are some possible differences between a believer who disobeys God and a believer who is characterized by disobedience?

8. What unchecked attitudes might lead to habitual disobedience?

9. *Thought question:* What positive principles for dealing with sin and its consequences might you draw from this lesson?

❧ *DIGEST* ❧

Every child disobeys, but not every child is characterized by disobedience. Correction is a vital part of obedience training. Through parental correction, children learn to obey. On the other hand, when a child consistently refuses to be corrected, he soon becomes characterized by disobedience. A stubborn, willful attitude cultivates unacceptable behavior patterns.

How like the believer's obedience pattern this is. In a moment of anger, strong desire, fear, or weakness, anyone of us might disobey God—and suffer the consequences. Unacceptable behavior can become a pattern, if negative attitudes remain unchecked.

Temptation follows temptation. Have you ever noticed that when you disobey God, you frequently face the immediate temptation to shift blame, rationalize behavior, question God's fairness, or discount his faithfulness? Succumbing to this temptation compounds the original act of disobedience and can lead to a pattern of disobedient behavior. How often have you seized one of the following ways to explain (or defend) an act of disobedience?

□ "It wasn't my fault." Blame-shifting is one of the most common responses to disobedience. It's difficult to deal with sin in your life if you refuse to accept responsibility for it. While we recognize that outside influences and other people create difficult situations for us, we are still responsible for our own behavior.

□ "I know it was wrong, but it's not as bad as what a lot of other Christians do." Rationalizing is another common barrier to dealing with sin. God isn't concerned with how we measure up to the next person; He is concerned with our willingness to obey Him.

□ "God, this isn't fair!" Sin brings consequences—some of them quite painful. It is sometimes difficult to accept these consequences. We tend to blame God for the predictable results of our own disobedience. Unchecked, this attitude breeds bitterness.

□ "God doesn't care about me—He doesn't answer my prayers." Forgetting God's past faithfulness in a time of crisis was a major failing of the Children of Israel and contributed greatly to their pattern of disobedience. In God's eyes this was a grave sin (Num. 14:11). When we discount God's past faithfulness, we feed the cycle of bitterness.

Two response patterns. Deuteronomy clearly sets forth two response patterns in dealing with disobedience. The saga of Israel in the wilderness is a history of rebellion in the making. Israel continually refused to be corrected. She compounded disobedience by rationalizing, refusing to accept responsibility for action, and discounting God's past faithfulness.

Israel's negative pattern is contrasted with Moses' positive pattern. Moses had spent much of his time teaching the Israelites "If you disobey God, there will be consequences," before he also disobeyed God. Both Moses and the rebellious generation died in the wilderness. But there the similarity ends. Like Israel, Moses could have rationalized his sin. He could have said, "The people made me so angry I couldn't help myself." But he didn't. His life did not become characterized by sin. After his disobedience he saw many years of fruitful service and he enjoyed an ever deepening relationship with God.

Two choices. The Bible has no perfect heroes. It is full of examples of imperfect people who found life after failure. It is also full of examples of people who became totally entrenched in disobedience because they refused to deal with sin in their lives.

Saul and David present this contrast. Both disobeyed God. Both suffered consequences for their sin. One accepted God's correction. One stubbornly persisted in having his own way. Saul became characterized by rebellion. David became a man after God's own heart.

Psalm 51 is an excellent prayer model for those who desire to develop obedience behavior patterns. If you are facing a problem with disobedience, use this as a prayer to correct attitude and action.

> Have mercy upon me, O God, according
> to Thy loving-kindness; according unto
> the multitude of Thy tender mercies
> blot out my transgressions.
> Wash me thoroughly from mine iniquity,
> and cleanse me from my sin. For I
> acknowledge my transgressions: and my
> sin is ever before me.
> Create in me a clean heart, O God;
> and renew a right spirit within me.

Psalm 51:1-3, 10

❧ MOMENTS OF DECISION ❧

Can you think of a time when you disobeyed God and then responded to the consequences by rationalizing your action, discounting God's love/care for you, calling the consequences unfair?

Are you still responding in this manner? How might the pattern be changed?

Write out a prayer expressing any decision you have made as a result of this lesson.

CHAPTER TWO

A Repentant Heart

❧ DISCOVERY TIME ❧

1. Read Deuteronomy 4:23-31 and then outline the passage following the steps below.

   The passage may be divided into three major sections (listed below): scan the passage, find these sections, and write the reference beside each section heading below.

   Under the first section heading, list the specific elements of Moses' warning. (**Note:** You should have two or more.)

   How many specific consequences of Israel's disobedience can you find? List these under the second heading.

   Find three separate actions which determined conditional restoration and note them under the third heading.

   Warnings against disobedience

   Consequences of disobedience

   Conditions of restoration

2. *Thought question:* Which of the consequences would most likely be a constant reminder of Israel's sin? Explain your answer.

3. Who are the two witnesses Moses calls upon in verse 26?

4. Read Deuteronomy 8:10-20, noting specific attitudes or actions mentioned in this warning. Specifically what is Moses warning against in Deuteronomy 8:11-17? Try to think of one word or one phrase which identifies the sin he is warning against.

Write a summary of the warning in this passage.

5. What admonition is found in verse 18 for those who may be tempted with pride over material possessions?

6. In chapter 30, God promises restoration to repentant Israel. Read Deuteronomy 30:1-6, especially noting promises for conditional restoration for the disobedient nation. Summarize the conditions of the restoration in the columns below. Be thorough.

God promises to do this: *If Israel will do this:*

7. Read the following verses. What promises or instructions do you find for New Testament believers in need of restoration?

1 John 1:9

Revelation 3:19

Galatians 6:1

8. Think about the warnings to Israel you have discovered in this lesson. In what areas might New Testament believers need similar warnings? Be specific.

9. Recall some of the actions required in repentance that leads to

restoration. What is required of both Israel and of Christians who need restoration?

10. *Thought question:* Why do you think that Moses presented these three themes (don't disobey; if you do disobey, God will discipline; when God disciplines you, repent and turn back to Him) together in one message?

❧ *DIGEST* ❧

One woman, writing of her struggle with sin, tells of coming to a place where she declared, "I've gone too far this time, I've really hit bottom. Even Jesus Christ can't help me now." Her friend wisely responded, "With Jesus, there is no bottom."

It is true that God hates sin and He will not allow His children to flagrantly disobey Him. But it is also true that God loves the sinner. He stands ready to restore the truly repentant. These two facts go together.

Disobedience judged. Moses spent much of his last thirty days warning the Israelites about the high cost of disobedience. Foreseeing their occupation of the land, he warned them not to forget God. Particularly he warned against the sin of turning to other gods. Such sin would surely result in their being cast out of the land. The suffering which follows Israel's disobedience is recorded in terrible detail in Deuteronomy 28: barren wombs; barren fields; barren livestock; drought; disease, plague, madness, blindness; fear, panic, confusion; defeat in battle; siege, captivity; forced worship of stone/wooden gods; laughingstock of many nations; want of all things; and despair of life. Nothing could be clearer—God would judge and continue to judge those who persisted in disobedience.

Repentant Forgiven. Moses did not leave the people without hope. In chapter 30 he gives the other half of the message—even in their captivity, if they would turn back to God—even there He would hear them. True repentance would lead to true restoration. To the repentant He promised compassion, regathering from captivity, possession of the land, fruitful wombs, and fruitful endeavors.

In his book *Forgiving Is For Giving,* Jason Towner identifies God's greatest gift as forgiveness, and points out that forgiveness has always been "on God's agenda."

Towner reminds us that every possible act of depravity is recorded in God's Word including rape, murder, and homosexuality.

According to Towner, the Holy Spirit deemed this record necessary in order that all may know such experiences are common to human-kind and that there is no human experience which is beyond the healing power of Jesus Christ.

The whole message. God's statement about sin does not vary. He hates sin and will judge it; He loves the sinner and will forgive the repentant. It's a whole message. It should be preached as a whole, understood as a whole, accepted as a whole, and acted upon as a whole.

We cannot respond correctly unless we respond to the whole mes-sage. If we respond only to the fact that God loves the sinner, we easily presume upon that love. On the other hand, if we respond only to the fact that He hates sin, we just as easily deny ourselves the love that He offers.

A proper response. We dare not take the recourse of repentance lightly. It does not allow for willful living interspersed with perfunctory mutter-ings of "I'm sorry, God. I'll try a little harder." Nor should we reject the recourse of repentance because we assume we have "come to the bottom." We must remember that even there God hears the repentant.

True repentance involves recognition of wrongdoing and turning from it. While some might labor over an exact formula for repentance, we profit most by recognizing the bottom line: God knows our hearts, He recognizes the truly repentant.

The believer's hope. John writes of sin and repentance in his first letter to New Testament believers. In this letter John acknowledges:

☐ *Believers do sin* (1 John 1:8—2:1).

☐ *Sinning believers have an advocate pleading for them* (1 John 2:1).

☐ *Sinning believers have the recourse of repentance* (1 John 1:9).

☐ *Our own hearts may condemn us but God is greater than our hearts and knoweth all things* (1 John 3:20).

John would have agreed: With Jesus Christ, there is no bottom. True repentance leads to true forgiveness and restoration.

❧ MOMENTS OF DECISION ❧

What is the most important thing you learned about sin? Repentance?
Restoration?

What part of the lesson helped you most?

How can you apply it to your life this week?

CHAPTER THREE

A Healed Heart

🙢 DISCOVERY TIME 🙢

1. Read 2 Samuel 12:1-24. What was David's sin?

   What did David say when confronted with his sin?

   What phrase indicates God's forgiveness?

   What consequence of David's sin is recorded in this passage?

2. Read Numbers 20:2-13. Describe the pressures confronting Moses in this scene (vv. 2-5).

What specific instructions did God give Moses and Aaron? (v. 8)

How did Moses disobey God? (vv. 10-11)

What was the consequence of his disobedience? (vv. 12-13)

3. Read Deuteronomy 3:24-28. In chapter 1 you read this prayer which Moses prayed in hopes that God would take away the consequence of his sin. How did God answer Moses' prayer?

4. Now read Deuteronomy 31:1-2 and 32:48-52. How long did Moses live with the consequence of his sin?

5. Sometimes we endure consequences not of our own doing. In the following questions you will discover how Caleb was affected by the disobedience of others.

Read Joshua 14:6-13. What incident is Caleb recalling? (vv. 6-8)

How had Caleb's past action differed from that of his fellow spies? (v. 8)

How many years did Caleb bear the consequences of someone else's sin? (cf. vv. 7, 10)

What promise had Moses made to Caleb? (v. 9)

In what way does Caleb testify of God's faithfulness?

6. Note the response of all three men to the fact that certain consequences could not be reversed. Each continued to worship God and

to serve Him to capacity throughout their lives.

In the following passages find what was said about Moses and David after their deaths.

Deuteronomy 34:10

1 Kings 14:8

7. What do you think are some of the problems people encounter when facing consequences of past action? On a scale of 0 to 10 (0 representing no problem, 10 representing a severe problem), rate the following list of potential problems.

                        0   1   2   3   4   5   6   7   8   9   10

Anger at God

Anger at others

Guilt over the past

*A feeling of being
   unforgiven*

*A feeling of being
   on the shelf*

Defensiveness

Coldness

Withdrawal from God

Withdrawal from others

8. What principles from the lives of David, Moses, and Caleb would be most helpful in avoiding these problems?

9. *Thought question:* Read Deuteronomy 33:26-29—Moses' very last words to Israel before he died. Considering what you know about Moses, what do you think these words reveal about the one who spoke them?

🍂 DIGEST 🍂

When I was a young girl, I fell against a wood-burning stove. As a result, for many years, I carried the flower design of that stove on my side. Over the years I have also accumulated numerous surgical scars. These scars serve as a reminder of past illnesses but they reveal nothing about my present state of health. In no way do they indicate a lack of healing.

In much the same way as scars, certain consequences of past sin may be with us for life. If the past action has been dealt with, God has forgiven that sin. He does not, however, always take away the consequences.

Facing the consequences. Many believers allow such consequences to overshadow their relationship with God. They live with guilt and/or discouragement over past action which has changed the course of their lives. Daily they face the painful question, "Now that I've blown it, how can I ever be the person God wants me to be?"

Moses is an excellent model of one who faced this question with positive results.

Everything we read about him from Numbers 20 through the end of Deuteronomy took place after Moses' great failure which resulted in irreversible consequences.

It happened at a place called Meribah. (You can read about it in Numbers 20.) The people were out of water and Moses was out of patience. After years of faithfully following God, Moses grew impatient, lost his temper, and struck the rock twice, completely disregarding God's specific order to "speak to the rock."

The needed water came. But God spoke at that point and declared that Moses would never lead the people into the land. His sin resulted in irreversible consequences, yet the record shows that he continued to make obedience his goal. For some, a Meribah experience is where it all ends. For Moses it was simply another beginning.

Loving the God you failed. Through carefully reading Deuteronomy, we see that Moses' relationship with God continued to deepen. He continued to love and to serve the God he had failed.

Some clues to Moses' love for God are found in the last chapters of Deuteronomy. There Moses says of God:

☐ *There is none like God.*
☐ *He will not fail.*
☐ *He will not forsake.*
☐ *He is the Rock.*
☐ *His work is perfect.*
☐ *He is a God of truth.*
☐ *He is just and right.*

Even his attitude toward Israel indicates a deep relationship with God, for he did not see Israel as the constant source of grief they had been. Instead he saw them through God's eyes—a unique people chosen by a unique God. Of Israel, Moses said:

"Who is like unto thee, O people saved by the Lord!" (Deut. 33:29)

Perhaps the greatest clue concerning his ongoing relationship with God is the epitaph recorded in Deuteronomy 34:10. There Moses is identified as a unique prophet:

"There arose not a prophet since in Israel like unto Moses, whom the Lord knew face to face."

The truth about consequences. If you are living with irreversible consequences of the past, consider two important truths:

☐ 1 John 1:9 assures us that if we confess our sin, God is faithful and just to forgive us that sin. Past action is forgiven even when the consequences of that action remain. Such consequences do not indicate a lack of forgiveness any more than scars indicate a lack of healing.

☐ We are called to faithfulness, not perfection. It was Moses' faithful pursuit of God, not his perfection which made him unique. He began again, continued to love, continued to obey, and continued to seek God's direction.

Moses didn't waste emotional energy trying to recapture the past. Nor did he reflect unnecessarily on what might have been, had the incident at Meribah never taken place.

The simple truth about consequences is that while some may be with us for life, serving as painful reminders of the past, they say nothing about the present spiritual condition of the individual.

❧ MOMENTS OF DECISION ❧

If you are dealing with consequences of the past, use one of the following suggestions to get you started in your journal.

Write yourself a reminder that consequences of the past have nothing to do with present spiritual condition.

Choose a principle which you learned and write out how you will apply this to avoid problems in dealing with consequence.

If you have a friend who feels defeated because of the consequences of past sin, write out a prayer for her. Pray specifically that she will know restoration in spite of the consequences.

CHAPTER FOUR

🕭 DISCOVERY TIME 🕭

1. Chapter 3 established the fact that Moses lived with irreversible consequences of his sin. When he sinned at Meribah (Numbers 20), his expectation of entering the Promised Land was canceled. This chapter will focus on Moses' post-Meribah ministry. What did he do once he knew his options were restricted? What was his attitude toward God after he had "blown it"? What can we learn about serving and loving God even when we live with consequences of the past?

   Chart Moses' post-Meribah service by writing a brief summary of the information you find in the verses listed below.

   Military Conquests

   Numbers 21:1-3

   Deuteronomy 2:31-33

   Deuteronomy 3:1-3

Conquest/Division of Land East of Jordan

Deuteronomy 3:12

Deuteronomy 3:13

2. Moses' most powerful oratory was delivered after his sin at Meribah. Knowing he could never realize his highest dream, Moses could have focused on "what might have been" and how the stubbornness of the Israelites had contributed to the situation. Instead he focused on the person of God, and His past, present, and future care of Israel.

In the following verses, find what Moses said about God's past care for Israel.

Deuteronomy 1:30

Deuteronomy 1:31

Deuteronomy 1:33

Deuteronomy 2:7

Deuteronomy 10:21-22

3. Which phrases in the following verses indicate Moses' confidence in God for the future?

Deuteronomy 31:3

Deuteronomy 31:4

Deuteronomy 31:5

Deuteronomy 31:6

Deuteronomy 31:7

Deuteronomy 31:8

4. Search Deuteronomy 32:4, 6 and see how many distinct phrases about the person of God you can discover.

5. Remember that Deuteronomy is Moses' final message to Israel. He knows he will die soon. What he speaks here are his last words. On the basis of his last instructions, how would you describe Moses' relationship with God at this period of his life? Explain your answer.

6. What contemporary application do you see from this lesson?

🎜 DIGEST 🎜

Author William Least Heatmoon said of a writing project, "The idea came to me on February 17, a day of canceled expectations."

It has often occurred to me since reading that statement, that the book of Deuteronomy was also a book written out of canceled expectations. At the time Moses wrote this book, he was fully aware that his most cherished goal—his expectation for the future—had been snatched away. He had, in fact, disqualified himself from pursuing the goal.

Dreams die hard. At one point in time, Moses attempted to persuade God to reconsider, but God declared the subject closed. And Moses accepted God's decision. He knew that the last word had been spoken. He would bear the consequences of his sin through the rest of his life. He entered into a new season in life.

The post-Meribah years may best be described as the detour period of Moses' life. Disqualified from pursuing his goal, he pursued other goals. Barred from leading the Israelites into the land, he prepared them, and his successor, for the entry. What can we learn from Moses about serving God in the detours of life?

Obey—a present tense word. Moses determined to obey God. Before the incident at Meribah, he preached, "Obey God." After the incident at Meribah, he preached, "Obey God." He recognized that in a moment of great temptation, he had failed God. But he also recognized that obedience is an ongoing commitment. There may be setbacks, but a heart for obedience continues to make obedience the goal.

Failures may bring about detours. But He who is Lord on the main road, desires to be Lord on the detour.

Redirected—not shelved. Moses continued to serve God wholeheartedly. While he was restricted in his service, he was in no way "on the shelf." True enough, he could not lead the Israelites into the land. But he led them in important military victories; allocated land East of Jordan to ¼ of the nation; trained his successor; and thoroughly prepared the nation for occupation.

Detours are not dead-end streets. There is a temptation accompanying restricted ministry to throw up one's hands and say, "I've spoiled it all. I can never do what God really intended me to do. What's the use?" In such preoccupation with what can never be, our eyes are blinded to that which can be.

A woman once confided in me her deep desire to be a pastor's wife. She dreamed of serving side by side with her husband, leading a congregation. Her joy in the Lord was dimmed by the realization that irreversible consequences of the past made this impossible. In their theological circle, both she and her husband were disqualified from this, her most cherished goal. For a time the sting of regret over what could never be, clouded her vision for what could be. But in time, she accepted the fact that while certain areas were closed to her, many others were open. She (and her husband) caught a new vision. In fact, God used this couple in an extraordinary way to reach a group of professionals to whom no minister had access.

A greater goal. When one studies the entire life of Moses (Exodus through Deuteronomy) it becomes apparent that somewhere along his journey obeying God became Moses' most important goal. In his earlier life he questioned whether he could do the job God wanted him to do. But he obeyed. It seems obvious that his obedience did not come from years of loving God, rather his love for God came from years of obeying Him.

Two contemporary songwriters have expressed this. Bill Gaither writes, "The longer I serve Him, the sweeter He grows." Mark Pendergrass declares, "The greatest thing in all my life is loving/serving You."

If you struggle over that which cannot be, remember Moses' example. He lost the opportunity to achieve an important goal. But he never lost sight of the greater goal. For that reason, his detour never became a dead-end street.

MOMENTS OF DECISION

Are you facing a spiritual detour? If so, consider one or more of the following journal suggestions to help you make it a productive time in your life.

Thank God for forgiveness of sin.

Make a list of ways in which you can express your love and obedience to the Lord. Include specific ways you can serve Him at this time.

Remind yourself of His past faithfulness by writing out some examples of His care for you.

Write a short poem of praise or a note to God expressing your love and your desire to obey Him today.

CHAPTER FIVE

Heart Attitudes

❦ DISCOVERY TIME ❦

1. Read Deuteronomy 5:22-33 several times if necessary in order to visualize the incident Moses is recalling. Think through the people's actions/responses to what they saw. What event was Moses recalling? (v. 22)

What had the people seen? (vv. 23-24)

How would you describe the people's reaction? (vv. 25-26)

What did the people promise? (v. 27)

What is the most probable motivation behind the promise?

According to God's response, what was the key to the people's obedience?

2. It is important to see the different meanings of fear. Fear is alarm and dread. Fear is also a profound reverence for God. The first definition is a weak motivation for obedience, the second is a strong motivation. The Israelites felt alarm and dread because of what they saw and this motivated them to make a promise. But because they lacked the reverential fear, they were unable to fulfill that promise.

According to Deuteronomy 5:29, what is the key to obedience?

How is both attitude and action involved in Deuteronomy 6:3?

How does Deuteronomy 6:5-6 show that action begins in the heart?

3. In the following references, find two negative attitudes and possible results of these attitudes.

Deuteronomy 7:17-18; 20:8

Deuteronomy 9:4-5

4. Mindset, disposition, inclination are all synonyms for attitude. The many references to the heart, as it pertains to action, remind us that heart attitudes affect action. Fear, reverence, and pride are easily understood as attitudes; it is important to see that loving, observing, and hearing are often actions which begin with the right attitude.

Read Deuteronomy 10:12. Write out the question in this reference.

What is the answer to this question?

NOTE: The expected response to Deuteronomy 10:12 is found in 10:16. In verses 13-15, Moses reminds the people that all heaven and earth belong to God and yet God chose Israel to be His special people. In verse 16 Moses urges them to circumcise the "foreskin of your hearts." Circumcision was the physical sign of the covenant with Israel. But Moses is pointing to the fact that an outward action (cutting off the foreskin) is not enough. A change of attitude was needed.

5. What thoughts concerning obedience can you find in the following passages:

Proverbs 4:23

Matthew 12:34, 45; 15:19

John 14:21, 24

Ephesians 4:17-19

6. Read and compare the following verses before answering the questions: Deuteronomy 6:5; Matthew 22:37-40; Romans 13:9-10. What did Jesus call the first and greatest commandment?

Since this is not the first of the Ten Commandments (Ex. 20:3-6), what do you think He meant?

How does Paul tie attitude to action in the Romans passage?

7. In Deuteronomy 30:17-20 Moses concludes his message on the Law by showing once again the relationship between heart and action (v. 17). He shows them the choice is between death and life and urges them to choose life.

What three actions follow the positive choice for life? (v. 20)

How does this apply to contemporary believers who struggle with obedience/disobedience?

❧ DIGEST ❧

"He has a terrible attitude."

"She has a good attitude."

These statements on a job application can be crucial to the outcome of the procedure. If a bad attitude is cited, one may expect to find a person who tends to be sullen, defensive, self-centered, hostile, uncooperative, or unteachable. She may be naturally talented, highly skilled and experienced, but a negative attitude can turn an otherwise qualified person into a poor employee.

On the other hand, "She has a good attitude" can be a positive plug to give a chance to a person who is somewhat lacking in experience or advanced skills. A proper attitude usually means the employee will be teachable, cooperative, and conscientious.

As attitude is related to action, so changing one's attitude is related to changing one's action.

A matter of the heart. In the Scriptures we find many references to the heart as the key to action.

Jeremiah declares, "The heart is deceitful and desperately wicked" (Jer. 17:9).

David prays, "Create in me a clean heart" (Ps. 51:10).

God declares of Israel, "O that there were such a heart in them that they would obey Me" (Deut. 5:29).

Moses reflects concerning Israel, "God has not given you a heart to understand, eyes to see, ears to hear" (Deut. 29:4).

Clearly, if Israel was to obey, her heart had to be in the right place.

Identity of the heart. Moses admonished the Israelites to "circumcise the foreskin of your heart and be no more stiffnecked" (Deut. 10:16). Freely translated he is saying, "In your heart, identify yourself with God and quit being so stubborn." Physical circumcision identified the Israelites as God's chosen people. But Moses points out that to be truly identified with God demands a choice of the heart.

The physical identity failed to produce positive action on Israel's part. Heart identity is cited as the motivating factor for turning from negative to positive action. ("Quit being so stubborn") Positive action stems from a heart that has chosen to be identified with God.

A change of heart. Changing the heart involves controlling the thoughts. In Philippians, Paul admonished believers to think on things worthy:

☐ *Things that are true*
☐ *Things that are honest*
☐ *Things that are just*
☐ *Things that are pure*
☐ *Things that are lovely*
☐ *Things that are of good report*
☐ *If there be any virtue, if there be any praise, think about these things.*

This is not a case of mind over matter. It is the law of sowing and reaping. While we often refer to this truth with respect to controlling lust, we sometimes forget that all attitude is related to what goes into our minds. A bad attitude usually indicates that it is time to take inventory of one's thought life.

Feeding the heart determines what comes out of the heart. To feed the heart, one must be in the Word on an ongoing basis. Moses admonished Israel to bind the Word to their hearts (Deut. 6:8; 11:18).

Believers today must saturate themselves in the Word of God if they expect to effect a change of heart attitude. Through time in the Word we are constantly reminded of what God has done for us in the past, what God will do for us in the future, and how God expects us to respond. Without the constant input of the Scripture there can be little hope for inner change which leads to outer change.

To break a pattern of disobedience requires both a change of attitude and a change of action. For both Israel and twentieth-century believers, when it comes to obedience we are talking about a matter of the heart.

❧ MOMENTS OF DECISION ❧

For your journal time this week concentrate on your own attitudes, positive and negative, which lead to action.

Decide what steps you can take to correct negative attitudes, increase positive ones.

CHAPTER SIX

A Trusting Heart

❧ DISCOVERY TIME ❧

1. Read the following passages and write down some ways Moses reminded the Israelites of God's past faithfulness.

   Deuteronomy 2:7

   Deuteronomy 7:6

   Deuteronomy 7:9

   Deuteronomy 10:22

2. In Deuteronomy 7:12-19, Moses encourages Israel with promises for the future, anticipates their fear, reminds them of God's past record of faithfulness. According to verses 12-16, what would God do for Israel?

What fear would keep Israel from obeying? (v. 17)

What would help Israel overcome fear? (vv. 17-19)

3. As Moses commanded the Israelites to obey, he cited reasons why they should obey. Find the motivation for obedience in the following passages. Record your findings by showing both the command and the motivation.

Deuteronomy 5:15

Deuteronomy 6:20-24

Deuteronomy 10:22–11:1

Deuteronomy 11:7-8

Deuteronomy 15:15

Deuteronomy 24:17-18

4. In the following passages locate the promises for the future and the conditions of their fulfillment.

	Promise	Condition

Deuteronomy 11:11-15

Deuteronomy 11:24

Deuteronomy 31:3-6

5. In what ways do the following passages indicate that God's faithfulness should motivate New Testament believers to obedience?

Ephesians 4:32–5:2

Philippians 3:20–4:1

Colossians 3:1-2

6. Read Colossians 1:9-14 and analyze the passage by answering the following questions.

What did Paul pray for these believers?

What act of obedience is he demanding?

From what source would the believers receive power to obey?

What has God already accomplished in behalf of believers?

7. What record of past faithfulness or promise for the future do you find in the following passages?

Romans 5:8

Romans 8:32

Romans 8:38-39

Philippians 1:6

Philippians 4:7

Philippians 4:19

James 1:5

1 Peter 5:7

1 John 2:25

8. What do you think motivates people to obey God? On a scale of 1 to 10 (1 meaning hardly ever, 10 meaning almost always), rate the following motivations.

	1	2	3	4	5	6	7	8	9	10

Fear

Guilt

Natural desire to be good

A knowledge of God's promises to those who love Him

Love for God

Reverence for God

Acknowledgment of God's faithfulness

Other

9. In light of what you have discovered in this lesson, what correlation do you see between a knowledge of God's faithfulness/promises and cultivating a heart for obedience?

10. What are some ways contemporary believers can develop an awareness of God's past faithfulness and of His promises for the believer?

❧ DIGEST ❧

Track records, batting averages, report cards, résumés, all of these are keys to predicting performance ability. You may expect someone to perform at a certain level on the basis of past performances. Accurate records provide accurate clues as to what might be expected.

One of Moses' major themes in Deuteronomy is the past blessings and mercies of God. "Remember what God has done," he reminded Israel over and over.

Another major theme is God's promises for the future. "God will do as He has promised," Moses declared again and again.

These twin themes are emphasized as sufficient motivation for obedience. "Obey God. Just look at what He has done for you. Obey God. Just listen to what He has promised to do."

Certainly God's "track record" made Him worthy of Israel's trust. They had seen His past performance in their behalf. How could they fail to trust Him? How could they not believe that He would always care for them in the future? Much of their disobedience stemmed from the fact that they totally ignored what God had done for them.

In Numbers 14:11 God asks Moses, "How long will it be before these people believe in Me after all the things I have done for them?"

In all their wandering they never learned to obey and/or trust God. They never even progressed to the point of asking for their needs, knowing that God would supply. Instead they murmured, complained, and stubbornly rebelled.

Someone has well said, "10,000 mercies are forgotten in one moment of privation." Certainly that is an accurate picture of Israel in the wilderness. Is it a picture of you? Do you easily forget what God has done? Perhaps you need to go back and read His résumé.

Begin with the price that was paid for your deliverance from sin. Check out the many promises made to New Testament believers: Provision for our needs; Grace for each moment; Strength for each day; An eternal dwelling place.

God's past performance in your behalf is a matter of record. So are His promises for the future. Together, these comprise sufficient motivation for trust and obedience. An unknown poet has expressed it well in verse.

The Rest of the Way
O fathomless mercy, O infinite grace
In humble thanksgiving the road
I retrace
Thou never hast failed me, my Strength
and my Stay;
To whom should I turn for the rest
of the way?
Through danger, through darkness, by
day and by night
Thou ever has guided and guided aright
I have trusted in Thee and peacefully
lay
My hand in Thy hand for the rest of the
way.
Thy cross all my refuge, Thy blood all
my plea
None other I need, blessed Jesus, but
Thee
I fear not the shadows at the close of
life's day
For Thou wilt go with me the rest of
the way.

❧ MOMENTS OF DECISION ❧

Use one or more of these suggestions to get you started in your journal.

Write a prayer to God thanking Him for past faithfulness. Name specific evidence of that faithfulness.

Write out a favorite promise from the Scripture which is especially meaningful to you right now.

Make a "help me" list noting areas where it has been difficult to practice obedience. Can you commit yourself to working in these areas with His help?

A Godly Heart

❧ DISCOVERY TIME ❧

1. Try to visualize yourself in Moses' place—at the end of his life, looking back over 40 years experience with Israel. In spite of the frustration involved, he sees them as a unique people chosen by a unique God.

   Read Deuteronomy 31:19-22. What was the last assignment given Moses before he died? Why did God ask him to do this?

2. What do you learn about the person of God from the song recorded in Deuteronomy 32? (cf. vv. 4, 6, and 18)

   What do you learn about His care? (vv. 9-12)

3. In other passages throughout the book, Moses points to the person of God. Discover what he says about who God is in the following passages.

Deuteronomy 4:31

Deuteronomy 4:39

Deuteronomy 6:4

Deuteronomy 10:21

Deuteronomy 33:26

Deuteronomy 33:27

Deuteronomy 33:29

4. Moses also points to the uniqueness of God by showing what God
   had done and would do for Israel. What are the past and/or future
   divine actions in these passages:

Deuteronomy 8:7-9

Deuteronomy 8:15-16

Deuteronomy 9:3

Deuteronomy 10:22

Deuteronomy 20:3-4

Deuteronomy 30:3

Deuteronomy 31:8

5. In the following passages, what does Moses say about the unique relationship between Israel and their God?

Deuteronomy 10:15

Deuteronomy 14:2

Deuteronomy 28:9

Deuteronomy 28:10

Deuteronomy 33:29

6. The New Testament believer also has a unique relationship with this unique God. What do the following passages tell us about God's person?

1 Thessalonians 1:9

Titus 1:2

1 John 1:5

1 John 4:16

What do the following tell us about our relationship with Him?

2 Corinthians 5:7

2 Corinthians 6:17-18

Ephesians 1:4

Titus 2:14

1 John 1:3

1 John 3:2

7. In Deuteronomy 30:6 God promised future Israel that He would do for them what they could not do for themselves. God also promises to do for the believer today what we cannot do for ourselves. Read 2 Corinthians 5:21 and 1 John 1:8-9. What new thing did you learn from this study about the person of God?

8. In what way could a better understanding of the person of God enable you to cultivate a heart for obedience?

❧ DIGEST ❧

What have you learned about cultivating a heart for obedience? Let's review seven things we have studied.

☐ *Deal with sin by acknowledging it. Never try to rationalize sin or shift blame elsewhere.*

There are two courses which confront every believer who disobeys God: acknowledge the disobedience and repent, or rationalize it and persist in going your own way.

Israel and Moses present contrasting examples of how people deal with disobedience. Israel became increasingly disobedient as she rationalized every disobedience and persisted in having her own way. Moses acknowledged his sin, repented of it, and continued to worship and serve his God.

We all have the potential for disobedience, but choosing to acknowledge one's disobedience rather than rationalize it, makes the difference between committing an act of disobedience and becoming characterized by disobedience.

☐ *Do not be defeated by past sin. Take the recourse of repentance and accept God's forgiveness.*

Every disobedient believer has the recourse of repentance. God makes it clear that He hates sin, but He loves the sinner. He will not allow a believer to flagrantly disobey Him, but neither will He forsake that one who repents. To cultivate a heart for obedience, remember the two things God says about sin: He will judge sin. He will restore the repentant sinner.

☐ *Do not be defeated by irreversible consequences of past sin. Accept the consequences along with forgiveness.*

Residual irreversible consequences must never be seen as a sign of withheld forgiveness any more than scars should be taken as a sign of incomplete healing.

Moses experienced full restoration in his relationship with God but the consequences of his disobedience remained. Past actions may result in consequences which will be with us for life, but those consequences should never be allowed to defeat the repentant believer. On the basis of God's Word, we know that we are forgiven.

☐ *Focus on what can be done, not on what can't be done.*

Meaningful service is possible for any believer, even those who live with irreversible consequences of the past. Sometimes irreversible consequences restrict the areas in which one serves (i.e., divorce disqualifies for ministry in many circles) but restriction should simply mean redirection. Instead of focusing on the restriction, look for new areas of service.

Moses provides an excellent example of this in that everything he accomplished after Numbers 20 was done with the knowledge that there were restrictions imposed upon him because of his disobedience.

He also provides an excellent example of one who continued to develop an ever deepening relationship with God even after his failure.

There can be life after failure, mistakes, wrong turns. Abundant life and fruitful service can—and should—be the goal of every believer. The past— whatever it may be—cannot dim those goals.

☐ *Check the correlation between attitude and action in order to correct negative action and encourage positive action.*

Breaking a disobedient pattern is essential for those who would seek the twin goals of abundant life/fruitful service. Two changes are necessary to break the pattern: a change of attitude and a change of action.

The importance of attitude in relationship to action is emphasized throughout the Scripture. Breaking the pattern of disobedience is both a matter of the heart (attitude) and a matter of the hands (action).

☐ *Reflect on past blessings and future promises to motivate continual obedience.*

Continued obedience can be a matter of the memory. Moses challenged Israel to remember what God had already done and to anticipate what He had promised to do. These two perspectives are sufficient motivation for continual obedience.

If we take inventory of God's past blessings and remember His promises for the present and the future, we will be more motivated to obey Him. His "track record" makes Him worthy of our trust and obedience.

☐ *Focus on the person of God and you will cultivate an obedient heart.*

If you want to cultivate a heart for obedience, get to know the One you have set out to obey. It is obvious that Moses more and more became preoccupied with the person of God . . . who God is, what He has done, what He was doing daily, what He had promised to do for the future, how He saw His people. Moses is a clear example of the fact that the more you know God, the more you love Him. To focus on the person of God is to cultivate a heart for obedience.

❧ *MOMENTS OF DECISION* ❧

What is the most important thing you have learned through these studies?

Review the decisions you have made. Write out any new commitment or renewed commitments.

CHAPTER EIGHT

A Contented Heart

❦ DISCOVERY TIME ❦

1. Read Psalm 90. This psalm is generally ascribed to Moses. As you move through the parts of this psalm, keep in mind Moses' background: he had known many dwelling places in his life; for 40 years he had aided Israel in a never ending search for shelter, food, and water; the chief "work of Moses' hands" had been to teach God's ways to the Israelites and to lead them. They stubbornly resisted both his teaching and his leading.

In what ways do the following verses refer to a place of shelter?

Psalm 90:1

Psalm 91:1-2

Psalm 91:9-10

Psalm 92:15

Deuteronomy 1:33 (KJV)

Deuteronomy 33:27

2. Identify some of the dwelling places Moses knew by looking up the following verses.

Exodus 2:1-2

Exodus 2:3

Exodus 2:10

Exodus 2:15, 21; 3:1

3. According to Deuteronomy 6:10-12, what future shelter did Moses anticipate for Israel?

4. Read Deuteronomy 33:27-28. What was Moses' last statement regarding shelter, food, and water?

5. Read Psalm 90:14 in several different versions. Write a statement showing the relationship between satisfaction with God's mercies and joy.

6. What is the psalmist's declaration regarding God's faithfulness in Psalm 92:1-3?

7. Describe from the following passages, Israel's response toward God's mercies. Numbers 11:4-6; 14:2-4, 11.

8. Moses' teaching and leading the Israelites (the work of his hands) often appeared to be less than successful because the Israelites failed to respond properly. What does Moses pray regarding the "work of our hands" in Psalm 90:17?

9. What do you understand to be the key to contentment found in Psalm 90:14?

10. What are some possible reasons why we tend not to be satisfied with God's mercies?

11. How should the knowledge that God establishes the work of our hands affect our attitudes toward the successes or failures of our endeavors for Him?

❧ *DIGEST* ❧

There is nothing quite like a sudden confrontation with our mortality to remind us how often we take for granted the ordinary things which give evidence of God's faithfulness in our lives. Over the years flowers—even weeds—have come to symbolize all that I take for granted.

I recall one occasion which occurred during a time of personal illness. The doctor had been vague about what he expected to find when he scheduled surgery, but we knew the outcome could be serious. A few days before the surgery I spent an hour weeding the yard. The usual aversion to the chore was missing. I actually felt good that day to be doing what I was doing—pulling weeds under a too warm desert sun.

The surgery revealed nothing ominous. I recuperated quickly and soon recaptured my more normal attitude of "I hate to pull weeds." But in a very real way, I had been made aware of the fact that every day is a gift from God. Rain, sunshine, food, shelter, health, the beauty of His creation, the ability to enhance that beauty through weed pulling efforts are all mercies which we enjoy in the routine of life.

Our lack of contentment, according to Psalm 90:14, can be attributed to the fact that we have not learned to be satisfied with God's mercies. Often we allow the urgent to crowd out those little things which enhance our joy. All my life, daffodils have been a source of special delight. As a child growing up in the Midwest I called them "Easter lilies" because I didn't know any better. But by whatever name we called them, they were the first flowers to bloom. Because I always tired quickly of the long dreary winter season, I found the first flower of spring reason enough to celebrate. Since they are of such significance to me it should follow that I would surround myself with daffodils. Not so.

Planting season, spring or fall, always coincides with retreat season. Because of my traveling and speaking I find it easy to neglect many things, making promises to myself that next year it will be different.

Then, last year, I was once again confronted with the fact that every season is a gift from God and there are no guarantees of next spring. Suddenly the daffodil became a symbol of all the things I had neglected, the routine things of life taken for granted, the daily mercies unacknowledged.

It was the spring of the year when the doctor's ominous words invaded the routine of my life. Lymphoma! Hodgkin's disease! Radiation therapy! My first thought was "God, I just want to be around in June to see our daughter awarded her doctor's degree." It was a bit more rational than my second thought—"I haven't planted any daffodils for the last eight years."

I should have been responding in some way to the sober conversations with a team of doctors. Instead I continually returned to that one irrational thought, "It may be my last spring and I don't have any daffodils."

My husband, always the optimist, understood my irrational response to the situation. He did what any sensible husband would do—he went to the nursery and bought a tub full of daffodils in bloom (fifty in all) and set them in my study. His note said simply "I don't ever want you to go through another spring without daffodils."

That was a year ago. While I continue in a rigid follow-up program, the prognosis is excellent and we seldom think about my bout with Hodgkin's disease. But I have not forgotten the lesson. On my table is a bouquet of daffodils. In my heart an acknowledgment of God's mercies and a prayer, "Satisfy me with Thy mercies that I may rejoice and be glad all my days."

One of the greatest lessons from Moses' life is his response to God's mercies. He experienced the same mercies, the same miracles as did the Children of Israel yet with a totally different response. They were never satisfied with the mercies of manna, shelter, water, or protection. Consequently they were a joyless generation.

Moses' relationship with God developed ever deeper throughout his life. He did not enter the land but he knew more joy and contentment than did the generation who occupied it. Not only was he satisfied with God's mercies, he was also content to leave in God's hands the ultimate results of any service he had offered. Whatever the future held for Israel, Moses died knowing that he had faithfully taught them God's ways. Only God could determine the results of his life's work.

❦ *MOMENTS OF DECISION* ❦

Use the following suggestions to get started in your journal.

Keeping in mind what you have studied in Psalm 90, what evidences can you see of God's faithfulness/mercy on your behalf? Write a list.

On the basis of Psalm 92:1-2, give thanks every day this week for the items on the list.

Write out Psalm 90:14. Memorize it.

🔊 *DIVERSIFY* 🔊

The following leader's guide provides you with specific suggestions to facilitate group discussion. You will find it most helpful if you encourage people to do the study before the group meeting. The objectives of this study are: first, to acquaint people with what the Bible actually says; and second, to show how the Bible applies to the practical problems of modern life. Go over the questions in class. Encourage discussion, but try to keep the discussion centered on the lesson, avoiding tangents. Remind group members that the more time they spend studying the lesson, the more interesting and informed the discussion will be.

As each session comes to a close, help group members discuss and draw conclusions that are practical and applicable to their individual problems. Also spend time sharing and praying for each other. This will increase the benefit each group member gains from this study.

General Guidelines for Facilitating
Good Group Discussion

☐ Encourage discussion by asking several group members to contribute answers to a question. "What do the rest of you think?" or "Is there anything else which could be added?" are two ways of doing this.

☐ Be open and warm toward all contributions. Never bluntly reject what anyone says, even if you think the answer is incorrect. Instead, ask what the others in the group think.

☐ As group leader, be sure not to talk too much yourself. Try to redirect questions which you are asked. A discussion should move back and forth between members. The leader is to act as a moderator. As members of a group get to know one another better, the discussion will move more freely.

☐ Don't be afraid of pauses or long silences. People need time to think about the questions. Never answer your own question—either rephrase it or move on to another area for discussion

☐ Watch hesitant members for an indication by facial expression or bodily posture that they have something to say and then give them an encouraging nod or speak their names.

☐ Discourage too-talkative members from monopolizing the discussion by specifically directing questions to others. If necessary, speak privately to the over-talkative one about the need for discussion, and enlist her help in encouraging all to participate.

General Guidelines for Group Leaders

Preparation

☐ Pray for the Holy Spirit's guidance as you study, that you will be equipped to teach the lesson and make it appealing and applicable.

☐ Read through the entire lesson and any Bible passages or verses that are mentioned. Answer all the questions.

☐ Become familiar enough with the lesson that, if time in the group is running out, you know which question could most easily be left out.

☐ Gather all the items you will need for the study: name tags, extra pens, extra Bibles.

The Meeting

☐ Start and end on time.

☐ Have everyone wear a name tag until group members know one another's names.

☐ Have each group member introduce herself or ask regular attenders to introduce guests.

☐ For each meeting, plan an activity (or ask an icebreaker question) to help group members get to know one another better.

❧ LEADER'S GUIDE 1 ❧

Objective
To lead group members to discover the difference between an act of disobedience and a life that is characterized by disobedience.

Personal Preparation
☐ Before you begin, read the introductory section.
☐ Complete the Discovery Time section of chapter 1.
☐ Read the Digest.
☐ Try to think of other illustrations (biblical and current) which show how people rationalize disobedience.

Group Time
☐ Ask the group to recall the details of the events they read about in the Scripture passage. Ask for a volunteer to begin, and then, as a group, recall as many details as possible.
☐ Encourage the group to discuss how people rationalize actions. Begin by asking the group to compile a list of recent news events which show people rationalizing negative actions.
☐ Ask: **What are some common situations in which we as Christians may be tempted to rationalize our actions?**
☐ Conclude the discussion by pointing out that it is human nature to rationalize our actions. But rationalizing also tends to make it easier to disobey again, so it's important to avoid it.
☐ Read Numbers 14:40-44 and be prepared to discuss the context and historical details of the passage, if necessary.
☐ Clarify any remaining questions over the distinction between disobedience and being characterized by disobedience.
☐ Ask one volunteer to share her thoughts regarding question 7. Then ask: **Did anyone come up with something essentially different which you would like to add?**
☐ Ask one group member to read her answer to question 8. Ask the group to share any additional attitudes from their lists.
☐ Ask for volunteers to read their answers to question 9. Allow ample time for each one to contribute the principles they have gained.
☐ Emphasize that the questions given in the journal are only suggestions to get them started. Clarify that each one is free to use this page in the way it is most helpful.
☐ Suggested prayer emphasis for closing: **"Lord, though disobedient at times, help us never to become characterized by disobedience."**

Leader's Notes

❧ *LEADER'S GUIDE 2* ❧

Objective
To help group members identify the action involved in repentance that leads to restoration.

Personal Preparation
☐ Complete the Discovery Time section for chapter 2.

☐ Scan Deuteronomy 27:11–28:68 (Blessings and Curses). The group members will not be asked to read this portion. But you will have a better grasp of the material if you familiarize yourself with the contents of this passage.

☐ Read the Digest. Jot down any further illustrations which may help group members to apply this lesson to contemporary situations.

☐ Pray for your group individually that each one may grasp both parts of the whole message in this lesson.

Group Time
☐ Emphasize the three themes and state that just as Israel needed this warning, each of us needs it today.

☐ Clarify any questions the group may have about the outline. While it is not important that all have the same division, a suggested division of the passage is:

    I. vv. 23-26
   II. vv. 27-28
  III. vv. 29-31

☐ Ask the group to list the three actions which determined conditional restoration. Then ask: **How do you think this adds to our understanding of repentance?**

☐ Encourage several to share the admonition they found for question 5. If they have not applied it to contemporary life, ask: **How do you think this admonition might be stated for Christians today?**

☐ Ask several to share their answers for questions 8, 9, and 10. Conclude the discussion by referring to the last paragraph of the Digest, "The Believer's Hope."

☐ If you have time, ask for sentence prayers expressing thanksgiving for the recourse of repentance.

Leader's Notes

❧ *LEADER'S GUIDE 3* ❧

Objective
To help group members identify ways to deal with the consequences of sin which may remain after repentance and restoration.

Personal Preparation
☐ Complete the Discovery Time in chapter 3. Make a note of the different types of circumstances/action which lead to consequences as you study the examples of David, Moses, and Caleb.
☐ Read the Digest. Underline any key sentences which will help you as you facilitate discussion of the lesson.

Group Time
☐ Ask the group to give their findings for questions 1 and 2. Encourage them to discuss any attitudes which may have contributed to the actions of David and Moses.
☐ Ask: **Can you think of one word which would describe David's sin? Moses' sin?**
☐ Encourage the group members that the next lesson will show how Moses lived a very productive life in spite of the consequences which remained with him.
☐ Ask the group to share any contemporary examples of how Christians may be caught in the consequences of another person's disobedience.
☐ Call attention to the statement in question 6. Point out that the examples given show three men who faced consequences for very different reasons. David's resulted from adultery, Moses' from anger, and Caleb's from another person's disobedience (many other persons).
☐ Allow ample time for the group to discuss how they rated this list in question 7. To help facilitate the discussion ask: **Which problem did you rate highest? How many agree with her? What other problem rated a high score?** When it becomes obvious which problems are rated the highest, ask: **Why do you think this is true?**
☐ Ask: **What principles might help you to avoid these problems?**
☐ Close with sentence prayers expressing love for the God who always loves us.

Leader's Notes

❧ *LEADER'S GUIDE 4* ❧

Objective
To help group members identify positive principles for serving God while living with consequences of the past.

Personal Preparation
 ☐ Complete Discovery Time Section.
 ☐ Read the Digest. Highlight the paragraphs "Obey—A Present Tense Word," and "A Greater Goal." These are key sections and you may wish to use one in closing the group discussion.
 ☐ Secure a copy of the songs, "The Longer I Serve Him," by Bill Gaither, and "The Greatest Thing in All My Life," by Mark Pendergrass. Bring them to class.

Group Time
 ☐ Allow the class to share the facts they gleaned from question 1. Emphasize the importance of Moses' work during this period of his life.
 ☐ Encourage group members to be specific as they share Moses' declarations about God's past care for Israel (question 2).
 ☐ After the group has shared their findings for question 3, ask: **What are some like promises that we have?**
 ☐ Ask: **When have you been especially reminded of a past blessing or a promise for the future?**
 ☐ If the group members have had a difficult time with question 4, use the question as a group exercise. Have Deuteronomy 32:4, 6 read in several versions. The *King James Version* has 11 distinct phrases referring to God in these two verses. Encourage members to keep trying until at least 6 or more are located.
 ☐ Ask for several volunteers to share thoughts on question 5.
 ☐ Ask: **How many found contemporary applications from this lesson? Who would like to share?**
 ☐ If time permits you may wish to share one of the highlighted paragraphs from the Digest.
 ☐ Refer to the two songs you have brought. If the group knows the songs, sing one. Otherwise share the words before prayertime.
 ☐ Close with a time of silent prayer.

Leader's Notes

❧ *LEADER'S GUIDE 5* ❧

Objective
To help group members pinpoint ways to bring about change in action through a changed attitude.

Personal Preparation
☐ Read and meditate on Proverbs 6:20-23. Write out a modern paraphrase of the passage.
☐ Examine your own heart. Pray that God will enable you to correct attitudes which may lead to negative action.
☐ Cut out hearts from a 4″ x 4″ square of paper to be used in prayer time. You will need one for each group member.

Group Time
☐ Discuss the probable motivation for the peoples' promise under question 1. The correct answer should be "fear." If they have not seen this, say: **Let's examine the passage again to see if we can discover another possible motivation.**
☐ Contrast *fear* and *love* as a motivation for positive action in (1) a marriage relationship; (2) a parent-child relationship; (3) one's relationship with the Lord.
☐ Ask someone to read Proverbs 6:20-23 to the group. Ask: **How is the law in the heart a "way of life"?** As a group, paraphrase the passage in contemporary language.
☐ Have the group share their answers to questions 6 and 7. Reinforce as needed, the correlation between heart attitude and action.
☐ Pass around the precut paper hearts. Ask each group member to write on her heart one positive attitude she would like to work on and then pass her heart to the woman on her right. Ask the group to pray for one another either by taking the requests home or leading in sentence prayers as you close.

Leader's Notes

❧ *LEADER'S GUIDE 6* ❧

Objective
To lead the group to a deeper trust in God's promises.

Personal Preparation
☐ Complete the Discovery Time section. Read the Digest.

☐ Try to recall an example from your own experience which shows that a person who stands behind his or her promises is a person others can depend on.

☐ Pray for your group members by name, asking God to help them catch a new vision of His faithfulness.

Group Time
☐ Introduce classtime by stating: **Remember, Moses is soon to die and he knows he will not enter the land. Still he is stressing God's faithfulness.**

☐ Ask group members to share their findings for question 1.

☐ Allow the group members to share findings for question 2. Ask: **In what way does Moses tie God's past care for Israel to His future faithfulness?**

☐ After group members have shared their findings for questions 3 and 4, say: **As New Testament believers we also should be motivated to obey as we reflect on God's past faithfulness. What are some things you learned about this from questions 5 through 7?** Allow ample time for members to share their answers to these questions.

☐ Discuss questions 8 and 9, allowing as many to participate as time permits.

☐ Reinforce any response to question 10 which points to studying God's Word and/or consciously reminding ourselves of His faithfulness on our behalf.

☐ Close in prayer, making your emphasis one of thanksgiving.

Leader's Notes

❧ *LEADER'S GUIDE 7* ❧

Objective
To encourage group members to develop a deeper relationship with
God through focusing on His person.

Personal Preparation
  ☐ Complete Discovery Time. Read the Digest.
  ☐ Try to recall an occasion when a Christian song served as a reminder
of God's faithfulness.
  ☐ Meditate prayerfully on question 6 and the passages involved. Pray
that you will have a new glimpse of your unique relationship with a unique
God.

Group Time
  ☐ After hearing answers to question 1, you may wish to share how a
Christian song has served to remind you of God's faithfulness at some time
in the past.
  ☐ Move carefully through these passages in questions 2 and 3. Point out
that Moses' preoccupation with the person of God is seen throughout
Deuteronomy.
  ☐ From question 5 bridge to question 6 by stating: **As New Testament
believers we also have a unique relationship with God.** Allow ample
time for question 6. Encourage specific answers. Reinforce answers which
clearly show who God is and what our relationship is with Him.
  ☐ After discussion on question 8, close by reading the final paragraph
from the Digest.
  ☐ Ask group members to close their eyes and think about who God is
and how He makes it possible for us to have a relationship with Him.
  ☐ Close with silent prayer.

Leader's Notes

❧ LEADER'S GUIDE 8 ❧

Objective
To lead group members to see the correlation between a contented heart and a satisfaction with God's mercies. To help them pinpoint God's daily mercies in their lives.

Personal Preparation
☐ Complete Discovery Time. Read the Digest.
☐ Meditate on Psalm 90:14. How does this speak to you in your own life?
☐ Secure magazine pictures of a house, a palace, and a tent. Take to group meeting.

Group Time
☐ Ask group members to take turns sharing their answers to questions 1-4. Pause at the end of each question and ask: **Did anyone have something essentially different?** If not, proceed to next question.
☐ After question 4, show pictures of a tent and a house. Emphasize that Moses had lived with Israel in the wilderness in tents and perhaps other crude shelter. He is now anticipating the immediate future when Israel will live in houses again. Show the picture of the palace and say: **The man who wrote Psalm 90:1 and Deuteronomy 33:27 left a palace to dwell in tents. What do you think his last words reveal about his contentment or lack of it?**
☐ Allow time for several members to share their answers to question 5.
☐ Discuss question 7. As answers are shared, lead them to see that Israel's lack of satisfaction is tied to discounting God's mercies in their lives.
☐ Encourage volunteers to share their answers to questions 10 and 11. These are key questions to personal application. Allow time for them.
☐ Ask group members to close with sentence prayers specifically acknowledging a daily mercy.

Leader's Notes